INTROD

Embarking on a journey to Sumatra is akin to stepping into a living tapestry of vibrant cultures, breathtaking landscapes, and untamed wilderness. As the author of this travel guide, I invite you to join me on a vivid exploration of an island that has not only captured my heart but has also left an indelible mark on my soul. Sumatra, with its rich tapestry of natural wonders and warm-hearted people, offers a journey that goes beyond mere sightseeing it is an immersion into a world where every moment is a discovery, and every experience is a treasure.

My journey through Sumatra began with a sense of anticipation that was palpable, fueled by stories of lush rainforests, majestic wildlife, and serene lakes that seemed too mystical to be real. Landing in Medan, the island's bustling gateway, I was immediately enveloped in the warmth of its people. Their smiles, as bright as the Sumatran sun, were a prelude to the genuine hospitality that would define my experience across the island.

Traveling from the north to the south, each destination unfurled its unique allure. The cool, misty mornings at Lake Toba, the world's largest volcanic lake, offered moments of serenity that felt almost otherworldly. Surrounded by the gentle lapping of the water and the panoramic beauty of the surrounding Batak highlands, I found a peace that was as deep as the lake itself. The traditional Batak houses, with their distinctive boat-shaped roofs, stood as proud sentinels of a culture that has thrived in harmony with nature.

In the heart of Sumatra, the dense rainforests of Gunung Leuser National Park beckoned with the promise of encounters with the island's famed orangutans. Trekking through this emerald labyrinth, the air alive with the chorus of the jungle, was a humbling experience that underscored the profound connection between humanity and the natural world. The sight of an orangutan, swinging with effortless grace through the trees, was a poignant reminder of the beauty and fragility of life on this planet.

Sumatra's west coast, with its legendary surf breaks and untouched beaches, was a testament to the island's raw,

SUMATRA

TRAVEL GUIDE

2024

Discover Culture, Nature & Adventure

JENNIFER JAMES

TABLE OF CONTENT

MAP OF SUMATRA

natural beauty. The Mentawai Islands, a surfer's paradise, offered waves that danced to the rhythm of the sea, challenging and exhilarating in equal measure. Here, amidst the ocean's embrace, the spirit of adventure was as tangible as the salt in the air.

Yet, it was not just the natural wonders of Sumatra that captivated me; it was also the rich tapestry of cultures that weaved through the island. In Minangkabau country, the matriarchal society's deep respect for its heritage was evident in the majestic Rumah Gadang, the traditional homes that speak of a community deeply rooted in its values and traditions. The Padang food, with its bold flavors and communal serving style, was a delicious insight into the region's culture, each meal a celebration of community and family.

The journey through Sumatra was also one of reflection, especially poignant in Banda Aceh. Standing amidst the remnants of the 2004 tsunami, I was moved by the resilience of the human spirit, in a community that, faced with unimaginable loss, chose to rebuild, remember, and look forward with hope. The Tsunami Museum, a powerful tribute to the lives lost and saved, offered a space for contemplation and remembrance.

This travel guide to Sumatra is more than just a collection of destinations; it is a mosaic of stories, emotions, and experiences. From the adrenaline rush of riding the waves to the quiet contemplation in a Buddhist temple, from the joyous laughter of children playing in a village to the solemn beauty of a traditional ceremony, Sumatra is an island that invites you to feel, explore, and connect.

To the intrepid traveler seeking the road less traveled, Sumatra offers a journey that will challenge, inspire, and change you. It is a place where adventure and discovery are woven into the fabric of everyday life, where each day brings a new story, a new friendship, and a new insight into the diversity and beauty of our world.

As you turn the pages of this guide and embark on your journey to Sumatra, I invite you to explore with an open heart and an eager spirit. Let the island's magic envelop you, let its beauty move you, and let its stories inspire you. Sumatra is not just a destination; it is an experience, a journey into the heart of what it means to explore, to discover, and to live.

With every step, let Sumatra reveal its wonders to you. Embrace the adventure, the connections, and the unforgettable moments that await. And may your journey through Sumatra be as enriching and transformative as it has been for me.

Welcome to Sumatra, where every journey is a story waiting to be told.

OVERVIEW

Within the Malay Archipelago, Sumatra is the second biggest island in the Greater Sunda group, after Borneo. The Sunda Strait divides it from Java in the south and the Strait of Malacca from the Malay Peninsula in the northeast.

North Sumatra, Jambi, Riau, West Sumatra, South Sumatra, Bengkulu, and Lampung are the seven provinces that make up the island, in addition to the Acehnese autonomous province. Medan, Palembang, and Padang are the main cities.

For daring travelers, Sumatra offers a plethora of unique and difficult experiences. It is an island of remarkable beauty.

Volcanoes, earthquakes, and tsunamis have changed much of the island, yet the people there appear to accept it all. Large cities, stunning beaches, deep rainforests, rushing rivers, and breathtaking landscapes may all be found here.

There are many different kinds of typical and uncommon rainforest animals on this amazing island. You may see

Sumatran tigers, rhinoceroses, elephants, and a variety of monkeys that hang from trees in addition to red-haired orangutans.

GEOGRAPHY AND CLIMATE

There are several separate areas within Sumatra, each with distinctive geographical characteristics. The western side of the island is dominated by the Barisan Mountains, which are home to many active volcanoes. The steep and hilly topography of the mountains lowers sharply to the Indian Ocean. Some of Sumatra's tallest peaks, including Mount Kerinci, the highest volcano in Indonesia at 3,805 meters (12,484 feet) in elevation, are found in this mountain range. On the other hand, Sumatra's massive palm oil and rubber plantations are concentrated on its eastern side, where low-lying plains and vast river systems have produced rich agricultural fields.

The Musi, Batanghari, and Indragiri rivers are only a few of the island's major river systems, which are essential for irrigation, transportation, and residents' means of subsistence. Sumatra is a well-liked travel destination for travelers looking for adventure and natural beauty because of its long coastline, which is home to stunning sandy beaches, mangroves, and coral reefs. Sumatra also offers abundant marine species.

The majority of Sumatra has year-round high temperatures and humidity due to its tropical rainforest environment. There are two distinct seasons on the island: the rainy season and the dry season. The heaviest rainfall occurs during the rainy season, which normally lasts from October to April. This is particularly true on the western half of the island, where the Barisan Mountains draw moist clouds from the Indian Ocean. The dry season, which lasts from May to September, is said to be the greatest period for exploration and outdoor activities since it has less rainfall.

With typical daytime temperatures ranging from 23°C to 31°C (73°F to 88°F), the tropical environment guarantees that temperatures stay mostly consistent throughout the year. Altitude may, however, have a substantial impact on temperature, with higher altitudes and mountainous areas experiencing colder weather.

CULTURAL INSIGHTS

On the thinly populated island of Sumatra, human settlements are few and far between, and nature grows wild. There was a time when the island was covered with jungle. However, agricultural production now occupies a large portion of the area. As a result, Sumatra's population is varied in terms of color and culture, with farmers making up the majority of them. For example, there are the Batak, who are high mountain people who live in the summits of Sumatra's volcanic highlands. These people have their unique traditions, architecture, clothing codes, and religious beliefs. Despite being a popular tourist destination, they see Lake Toba as their spiritual hub. Muslim in origin, the Mingangkabau culture is based in the town of Bukittinggi. Headhunters live on the island of Nias off the coast of North Sumatra. Even if stone-jumping is no longer a common habit, people still follow other old practices. In this tradition, young boys demonstrate their masculinity by leaping over a monument made of stone that is higher than two meters.

BEST TIME TO VISIT

The rainy season in Sumatra lasts from November to March. Here, the monsoons may be very strong, rendering roads impassable. In the west and southwest, you can also anticipate the sporadic occurrence of rain throughout the dry season. Traveling to Sumatra is most enjoyable from April through October.

TRANSPORTATION

GETTING THERE: AIR TRAVEL

The most popular method of transportation to Sumatra is via flight, and one of Indonesia's busiest airports is Kualanamu International Airport in Medan. Although it is quite a distance from the city center, a commuter rail service is available to get you there. The Sultan Mahmud Badaruddin II International Airport in Palembang and the Minangkabau International Airport in Padang are the two major airports. There are many local and international flights at these three airports. Numerous smaller airports exist in well, mostly serving domestic travelers.

Together with a wide range of domestic ferry services, there are several ferry services from Singapore and Malaysia.

Due to its immensity, flying is the most practical method to get across Sumatra. Although there a vast road network, travel times may be lengthy and traffic is often dense. Traveling around Sumatra is an experience in itself. Even simple trips take ages due to the poor quality of the roads. Long-distance bus travel may be difficult since Sumatran buses are made for tiny Indonesians, and I'm a big Westerner. On the other hand, you could feel completely at ease if you are smaller in stature. On the other hand, traveling by bus has the benefit of offering some breathtaking views while driving.

FERRIES AND SEA TRAVEL

From Java to Sumatra

Merak is the name of the harbor on Java's northernmost point. From Jakarta, you may go here via rail. Adjacent to the port lies the rail station. It will take three hours and cost around 10,000 IDR, however, they often only provide the lowest class. In addition, there are Damri Buses that connect Merak and Jakarta. Ferries go to the port of Bakauheni in Sumatra from this location. During the day, ferries leave every 20 minutes, and the trip to Sumatra takes two hours. Be advised that inclement weather may force the cancellation of boat services. Local buses to Bandar Lampung run from here (1:30–2h, about 30,000 IDR).

Other locations

Additionally, some ships connect Sumatra and other regions of Indonesia with Malaysia. The business, known as PELNI, or "Indonesian National Line," runs big cargo ships. For instance, links exist between Tanjung Balai Karimun (near Singapore) and Medan (Belawan port) from Batam (near Singapore). It takes twenty-two hours to do this trip. Tickets may now be purchased immediately at the dock or online. but often only a day or two beforehand. Purchasing PELNI tickets at one of their offices is the best option. View our instructions on using PELNI for travel.

Additionally, the Indomal Express runs between Dumai, Sumatra, Malacca and Port Dickson, Malaysia. For information about bookings and scheduling, see their website. Dumai is isolated from everything, however. It will take you at least 13 hours to reach Lake Toba from there.

Tanjung Balai in Sumatra and Port Klang in Malaysia are connected by the Aero Speed Ferry every Monday through Saturday. Once at Tanjung Balai, you may take a bus to Lake Toba (which takes four hours), a train (which takes five hours), or another bus to Medan.

Bus

You did read accurately. The state-owned public transportation bus operator in Indonesia, DAMRI, operates buses that go from Jakarta, Java, to Bandar Lampung, Sumatra's southernmost region. The bus traveled to Merak's harbor, boarded a ferry boat (you had to get off the bus here), and continued to Bandar Lampung.

Road Transportation: Vehicle Rentals and Buses

RENT A CAR

It is possible to hire a car in North Sumatra, and the majority of the cars have a chauffeur. Having your driver gives you total independence without the effort of figuring out the roads and signposts, and it's not as pricey as you may initially imagine. Most hotels can arrange for automobile rentals, including the Deli Raya Hotel on Jalan Balai Kota in Medan has self-drive cars for hire. Renting a vehicle is probably the most affordable option to go between the beaches on Pulau

Bintan since it is less expensive at Tanjung Pinang than it is at the Lagoi hotel resorts.

BUSES

Before taking a plane to Java, most tourists choose to take bus transportation to navigate North Sumatra, avoiding the unreliable road system in the south. While there are several bus links across Sumatra, certain areas may be quite hilly, with extensive forests, poorly maintained roads, and few bus connections. The little minibusses, often known as bemos or opelets, are always in demand. They are typically packed and reasonably priced. Certain minibusses provide a practical door-to-door service. Bus terminals Amplas (serving the south on Jalan SM Raja) and Pinang Baris (serving the north on Jalan Gatot Subroto) are located in the bustling city of Medan.

TRAINS

There's essentially just one train service that's worth mentioning for tourists on the island: trains that run between Bandar Lampung and Lubuklinggau via Palembang. Additional trains are available from Medan to locations including Pematangsiantar, Rantauprapat, and Tanjung Balai; however, residents mostly utilize this service, making it less helpful for visitors.

TAXIS

The largest airports in Sumatra provide taxi services, albeit most of them are a bit expensive. Taxis often make the 16-kilometer (10-mile) trip from the Sultan Iskandar Muda Airport to Banda Aceh. Additionally, there are plenty of taxis between Sultan Thaha Airport and the neighboring city of Jambi City (8 km / 5 miles), Sultan Mahmud Badaruddin II Airport and Palembang.

TOP DESTINATIONS IN SUMATRA

MEDAN: THE GETAWAY TO SUMATRA

North Sumatra may be accessed via Medan, the third-biggest city in Indonesia. Medan is often berated by tourists passing through quickly as one of the least attractive towns in Southeast Asia, although those who stay a little longer tend to think better of the city. It's as chaotic as any Indonesian city, with plenty of traffic congestion and pollution, but it also offers more urban amenities than any other place in Sumatra.

The population of Medan is diverse, coming from all over the archipelago and beyond. Notable minorities in the city are Chinese and Indian, whose ancestors came before the Dutch, who left behind a few elegant examples of colonial architecture, a testament to the wealth created by the enormous plantations that still today cling to the west of the city, up the slopes of Bukit Barisan. The city has an adequate museum, some intriguing temples in its Indian Quarter, and some remarkable early 20th-century architecture. Stay put.

Even just soaking in the noise of Indonesia's third-largest city may be a strong incentive to stay for a while, even if there may not be much to see and do there.

1.Browse the North Sumatra Museum

Located 500 meters east of Jalan Sisingamangaraja, also known as SM Raja, on the southern side of the Bukit Barisan cemetery close to the stadium, is the spacious and well-informed Museum of North Sumatra. It provides information about the region's history and features several historical stone Buddhist sculptures and two Arabic gravestones dating back to the eighth century.

2. Take in the Medan Grand Mosque

The Grand Mosque of Medan, or Mesjid Raya, is one of the most recognizable structures in Sumatra, with its black dome. Its 1906 design has arched windows reminiscent of North Africa, blue tiles for the walls, and vibrant stained glass windows. The architect was Dutch.

3. Look for some magnificent buildings.

The center of colonial Medan was Jalan Brig Jend A Yani, near the northern end of Jalan Pemuda, where a few early 20th-century structures may still be seen.

SUMATRA TRAVEL GUIDE 2024

The exquisite two-story green and yellow Mansion of Tjong A Fie (no. 105), erected in 1900 for the leader of Medan's Chinese community; the huge, dazzlingly white headquarters of PT Perkebunan IX, a government-run tobacco firm; and the elegant Harrison-Crossfield Building, dating from the 1920s.

4.Take a stroll in the Indian Quarter

The oldest and most revered Hindu temple in Medan is the Sri Mariamman Temple, located west of the city. It is dedicated to the goddess Kali and was constructed in 1884. The biggest of its type in Indonesia, Kampung Keling, the Indian neighbourhood, begins at the temple.

The number of Chinese has been rising in recent decades, countering the decline in the Indian population. The biggest Taoist temple in Sumatra, Vihara Gunung Timur, is located nearby and serves as a reminder of the Chinese presence. Approximately 800 meters south of Sri Mariamman, its plethora of dragons, wizards, warriors, and lotus petals are hidden away.

Nicest places to stay in Madan

Southeast of Mesjid Raya is where you'll find the greatest lodging options in Medan. Nothing about this place will wow you; most hostels and motels are small or quite basic.

About Jisingamangaraja Lane

A string of passable, inexpensive motels may be found under the shadow of Medan's Grand Mosque and along Jl Sisingamangaraja's western edge. The best location to stay to see the city's attractions is this one.

The top accommodations in Medan

Are you trying to find a certain hotel? Look no further. The most well-liked backpacker destination in town is Pondok Wisata Angel, which offers tidy, air-conditioned rooms with fans. Friendly staff, delicious cuisine, and free wifi are available at the downstairs Angel Café.

A pleasant selection of small rooms is available at Residence Clean, an eco-friendly hotel near the Grand Mosque. Standard rooms may be a little dingy (ask for one with a window) and have a small, indoor mandi. Top-floor rooms offer air conditioning and TV. Enjoy a nice rooftop garden and excellent value dining at the downstairs café/restaurant, which also offers free wifi.

Sultan Homestay This cheapie is located right in the middle of the budget motels and offers very basic rooms with common bathrooms. Take a break from the heat in one of the upstairs rooms with air conditioning. Free wi-fi is available, the staff is courteous, and breakfast is provided.

Medan's top eateries and bars

Medan has its kind of outdoor dining where some vendors congregate in one area and set up tables and chairs. Then, servers distribute menus that include all of the cuisine that is offered by each stall. Travelers sometimes go bowling at Yuki Simpang Raya or have drinks at the Tavern Pub, a popular hangout for expats that also has live music, at night.

The top eateries in Medan

Cahaya Baru: The greatest Indian restaurant in Kampung Keling, with air conditioning and a clean atmosphere. Though there are a few South Indian favorites (like masala dosa) and regional cuisines, the menu is mostly North Indian (think veg or chicken thali). The vibrant décor, authentic flavors, and local clientele all come together to provide the impression that you are in Delhi.

Tip Top Restaurant is a long-standing establishment that has been providing European and Indonesian cuisine since 1934. It is half restaurant, part institution in Medan. Along with a wide variety of pastries and ice creams, the broad menu includes Western, Chinese, and Indonesian meals.

How to navigate Medan

Although normal angkots (minivans) and taxis are useful for longer trips, motorized becaks (rickshaws) are the most popular mode of transportation in Medan for tourists.

Angkots

the backbone of the urban transportation system; many have names in addition to numbers. The Medan Mall stop is more convenient for travelers, however, the major angkot station is located in Sambu, west of the Olympia Plaza.

Automated benches

An additional practical means of navigating the city center. Before departing, decide on a price.

Taxi

A taxi is a widespread and affordable mode of transportation that may be useful, particularly at night. Use metered taxis only.

LAKE TOBA: A VOLCANIC WONDER

Lake Toba is one of the amazing natural marvels of the globe. In the center of this enormous crater lake lies an island about the size of Singapore. Lake Toba, at 1,145 square kilometers and 450 meters below the surface, is almost like an ocean.

A Soothing Getaway

Toba is a great spot to unwind and take in the stunning, unspoiled landscape. Your cares will fade away as you relax and enjoy the view of the lovely mountains contrasted with the refreshingly clean lake. The lake's

29

lower elevation of 900 meters above sea level results in a milder temperature, providing a much-needed respite from the heat, humidity, and pollution of the city.

How to Travel There

Through Air

Two flying paths go to Lake Toba. The first route goes from Medan's Kualanamu International Airport to Siborong-borong, North Tapanuli's Sisingamangaraja XII International Airport (formerly Silangit International Airport). It's a simple ground trip to Lake Toba from there.

Taking a direct flight to Sisingamangaraja XII International Airport is the second alternative. Direct flights from Jakarta and other major cities to Sisingamangaraja XII International Airport are provided by certain carriers. Make sure to look up the timetable for the most convenient route for you!

Through Land

Public buses travel two routes, from Medan to Parapat or from Medan to Beratagi, and may get you there in less than six hours from Medan, which is located 176 kilometers distant from the town by Lake Toba.

Medan travel agencies may also set you up with a chauffeured rental vehicle. There is a public bus accessible if you are traveling overland from the south via Tarutung and Bukittinggi.

How to Navigate

Take in the wind in your hair and explore this stunning region of the globe by renting a motorcycle, just as the locals do. If you find yourself on Samosir Island, spend the day exploring by taking a drive around the island's perimeter. This route, albeit rocky and unpaved at times, provides some breathtaking lake vistas from the island's highest elevations. The ideal method to move about if you're staying in the well-known Tuk Tuk hamlet on Samosir is to take a stroll along the main street.

You may take in the spectacular natural beauty of Lake Toba in a variety of ways. Kayaking at Lake Toba, according to many, is an experience of a lifetime. Tongging - Silalahi (12 km - Easy), Tongging - Samosir (50 km - Medium), and Northern Circle (175 km - Demanding) are the three typical kayak itineraries that you may explore. Glamping (glamorous camping) is another way to enjoy the refreshing wind from the

31

lakeside area on The Kaldera Nomadic Escape. Located in Sibisa, Ajibata Sub-district, Toba Samosir Regency, it allows you to experience nature up close without sacrificing any of the inconveniences associated with traditional camping. Additionally, its opulent amenities, which include bubble tents, eco pods, bohemian-style tents, and a 300-person amphitheater, will spoil you.

Situated on the island of Samosir, the ancient town is protected from the outside by trees, bamboo fences, and clay fortifications. The hamlet is also home to many unique and authentic traditional houses, especially in Tomok, where there is a row of spacious wooden houses with striking saddle-shaped thatch roofs made of sugar palm fiber (called ijuk).

It is well known that the Batak tribe has a joyous culture. The Tor-Tor Dance is regarded as the most graceful of the others. Typically, this traditional dance is done at festivities like harvest season or wedding ceremonies. However, history claims that the Tor-Tor Dance is a ceremony meant to call forth spirits and "walk" them into the stone statues that were created as a representation of the ancestors.

In addition, the myth and legend surrounding the wooden puppet known as Sigale-gale have made it a popular tourist destination on Samosir Island due to its supernatural significance. The people there thought that Sigalegale could dance and lament on its own without any music. Sigale-gale can only be put in a coffin, according to certain people. Because the Sigale-gale dance is seen by the locals to be a means of transferring the deceased's soul to the hereafter, this statue is also often utilized in family funeral rites in the Samosir region.

If you're searching for mementos, you might want to check out Ulos, a painstakingly woven textile that serves as clothing as well as a valuable heirloom, status symbol, and ceremonial gift throughout a person's life cycle, from conception and marriage to death.

In addition, genuine wood sculptures are available in the gift stores. For all of you coffee enthusiasts, don't forget to get the delicious Arabica coffee beans known as Sumatra Mandheling.

BUKIT LAWANG: THE ORANGUTAN HAVEN

Situated on the eastern flank of Gunung Leuser National Park, one of the three national parks included in the UNESCO listing for the Tropical Rainforest Heritage of Sumatra, lies Bukit Lawang, which is part of the Indonesian UNESCO World Heritage Site. Bukit Lawang, whose name translates roughly as "door to the hills," is a refuge for orangutans. As such, many visitors go hiking there in the hopes of seeing the endangered Sumatran orangutans.

Sumatra's Bukit Lawang Orangutan Sanctuary offers a haven for threatened species to survive in their native environments. The Sumatran orangutan is seriously threatened with extinction. Additionally, Bukit Lawang, a section of Mount Leuser National Park, is the location for wildlife protection of orangutans.

Celebrated for its jungle adventure, this ecotourism also serves as the primary entry point to Mount Leuser National Park, home to several huge species of both flora and wildlife. Formerly, Bukit Lawang served as a rehabilitation facility for illegally seized orangutans, after which they were released back into the wild.

Any time of year would be a good time to visit Bukit Lawang. Rainy seasons should be noted near the end of the year, but don't worry about it preventing you from traveling; it usually only rains in the evening or at night. Consider visiting during Indonesian public holidays, when a large number of local visitors will swarm the hamlet, particularly on weekends.

Founded in 1973, the sanctuary served as a rehabilitation facility for orangutans who had been taken from the illicit pet trade or left orphaned. It offers these monkeys a secure setting in which to acquire the abilities required for wild survival.

The refuge is around 100 hectares in size and is close to the Bohorok River. It has a feeding platform where guests may see the orangutans as they come to eat fruits given to them by the workers of the sanctuary. To see wild orangutans in their native environment, visitors may also take part in guided walks into the nearby jungle.

The Bukit Lawang Orangutan Sanctuary plays a crucial role in protecting the critically endangered Sumatran orangutan, which is threatened by poaching and habitat degradation. Additionally, it is crucial to inform tourists about the value of conservation and the need to safeguard these famous monkeys and their natural environment.

Reasons to Think About Visiting the Orangutan Sanctuary and Bukit Lawang

One of the most intriguing and intellectual species in the world, the orangutan, is protected and conserved at Bukit Lawang, an Indonesian town in North Sumatra. The following are some reasons for thinking about going to Bukit Lawang and the Orangutan Sanctuary:

1. Get Up Close and Personal with Orangutans

Seeing the magnificence of the orangutan in its natural environment is the major reason to go to Bukit Lawang. A rare chance to get up close and personal with these intriguing animals is offered by the Orangutan Sanctuary. Guests may see the orangutans as they arrive to eat fruits that the sanctuary staff provides, and if they're fortunate, they could even get to encounter wild orangutans when on guided walks in the nearby jungle.

2.Participate in Conservation Initiatives

You are contributing to significant conservation efforts to save the critically endangered Sumatran orangutan and its environment by visiting the Orangutan Sanctuary in Bukit Lawang. For orangutans rescued from the illicit pet trade or left orphaned, the sanctuary offers a secure haven where they can develop the abilities needed to survive in the wild. Your visit to the sanctuary supports these initiatives and serves to increase public awareness of the value of conservation.

3. Discover the Enchantment of the Rainforest

Within the Gunung Leuser National Park, an area of Indonesia known for its biodiversity is Bukit Lawang. Explore the wonders of the rainforest and take in the many different animal species that call the sanctuary home, such as Sumatran tigers, elephants, gibbons, monkeys, and a wide range of bird species. A unique way to take in the natural splendor of the rainforest is via guided excursions into the jungle.

4. Discover the Cuisine and Culture of the Area

Tourists visiting Bukit Lawang get the chance to sample the local food and culture. The settlement is home to the Batak people, who are distinguished from other Indonesian areas by their distinct cuisine and rich cultural past. Tourists may partake in traditional Batak palm wine, Tuak, and experience regional cuisine like Arsik.

For those who are interested in learning about local culture and food, exploring the jungle, or conserving animals, Bukit Lawang is a must-visit location. In addition to offering a rare chance to interact closely with these interesting animals, the Orangutan Sanctuary in Bukit Lawang also supports significant conservation initiatives. Make plans to visit Bukit Lawang and take in the splendor of this paradise in Indonesia.

PADANG AND THE MENTAWAI ISLANDS: SURFING PARADISE

Situated 100 kilometers off the coast of Sumatra, the Mentawai Island group is made up of more than 40 islands. More than 500,000 years ago, the archipelago broke away from the continent. The Mentawai Islands are home to a distinct variety of flora and wildlife that are unique to Indonesia due to their isolation and the passage of time.

The majority of Mentawai's population resides on the islands of Siberut, Sipora, North Pagi, and South Pagi. Pulau Sipora serves as both the island chain's only airport and the headquarters of the regional administration. The biggest and most developed island is Pulau Siberut, but part of it is a UNESCO Biosphere Reserve.

Due to their somewhat off-the-beaten-path location, the islands of North and South Pagi get relatively few visitors. That being said, if you're up for the challenge and have access to a boat, you could go there.

Traveling to the Islands of Mentawai

There are two, maybe three, choices available to you if you choose to go to the Mentawai Islands. Flying into Rokot Airport from Padang is the easiest method to get to Mentawai. Susi Air uses a 12-seater aircraft to provide an erratic service to the islands. It's best to contact Susi Air to make your ticket reservation. Please let them know if you intend to bring your surfboard.

The ferry is a clear substitute for flying. On Siberut, some businesses provide a quick boat service from Padang to Tuapejat. It is a three-hour program. Daily services are provided to and from Padang. The Mentawai Fast service's boat schedule is available here, fittingly enough.

Accommodation Options on the Mentawai Islands

The majority of travelers go to Mentawai Lodge on the Siberut or Sipora islands. Popular hotel booking websites like Agoda don't have many hotel listings; in fact, the only one we could discover was for the little 4-star HT's Resort on Sipora. Airbnb offers a few additional choices for low-cost and moderately priced lodging.

How to Proceed While You're There

The majority of your time will likely be spent riding waves. That's fantastic that is, after all, the reason the islands are well-known! The top surfing locations in the Mentawai Islands are listed on this website, which is helpful if you're not sure which breaks to visit. Although it's not an exhaustive list, it includes the top locations.

There are many intriguing things to do outside of the sea, and most of them are cultural. This involves going to see shaman rites that are put on for tourists in Siberut and going on forest treks to find the endangered black-and-yellow siamang kerdil monkey, which is native to the Mentawai Islands.

BANDA ACEH AND THE TSUNAMI MUSEUM

The Aceh Tsunami Museum is open every day (except Friday) from 10.00–12.00 midday and 15.00–17.00 West Indonesia Time at Jalan Iskandar Muda Street in Banda Aceh. The Museum building has embraced the elevated Aceh House heritage while also having a projecting funnel that gives it a ship-like appearance.

Entering, one is greeted with a small hallway with water streaming from both sides and ominous rumbling noises that bring to mind the destruction caused by the 2004 tsunami. In addition, photographs of the dead, survivor accounts, and an electronic recreation of the Indian Ocean earthquake are all on display in the museum. The museum was built on two storeys for around IDR 70 billion. An open space on the first level acts as a reminder of the tsunami tragedy.

The first level has many areas that serve as a reminder of that sad day, including photo galleries taken before, during, and after the tsunami. Here are a few pictures, artifacts, and a diorama. Among the most famous dioramas depict fishing boats being struck by strong waves and hurriedly washing ashore. A photo of the PLTD Apung Ship, which was washed ashore at Punge Blang Cut after being swept away and dragged far inland, is also shown.

There is instructional material on the second level, along with a library, 4D area, simulation rooms, and a gift store. A model of the earth's crust and a structure resistant to earthquakes are two examples of the simulation on display here. A chamber with artwork and a diorama depicting the tsunami event is also available.

Arrive there

The Aceh Tsunami Museum is situated on Jalan Iskandar Muda Street in the center of Banda Aceh, close to the intersection of the clock tower and Simpang Jam. It is located close to Kerkhof Peutjut, the Dutch Cemetery, and the Blang Padang Field.

ADVENTURE AND ACTIVITIES

HIKING AND TREKKING IN SUMATRA

National Park Gunung Leuser: An Entrance to the Jungle

Trekking aficionados will find Gunung Leuser National Park, a UNESCO World Heritage site and part of the Leuser Ecosystem, to be one of the best places to go in Sumatra. With a total area of more than 7,927 square kilometers, the park is home to a wide range of habitats, such as high-altitude cloud forests and lowland rainforests. Hikers on Gunung Leuser have the exceptional chance to see some of the most famous animals in Sumatra, such as orangutans, gibbons, and even the elusive Sumatran tiger. Situated on the eastern boundary of the park, the Bukit Lawang region is a well-liked departure point for multi-day jungle treks, with trails ranging from strolls to strenuous climbs deep into the rainforest.

Mount Kerinci: The Roof of Sumatra

Peak conquerors will find that Mount Kerinci, Sumatra's tallest volcano at 3,805 meters (12,484 ft), provides one of the most difficult and rewarding journeys. Trekkers may expect breathtaking views from the top that spread over the island, with clear days displaying the Indian Ocean to the west and the enormous Danau Gunung Tujuh crater lake below. The ascent passes through green tea plantations, deep montane forests, and alpine meadows. The ascent, which usually takes two days to complete, calls for a strong degree of fitness and planning, but the views and feeling of accomplishment are unmatched.

Samosir Island and Lake Toba: A Cultural Journey

Trekking around the world's biggest volcanic lake, Lake Toba, and its center island, Samosir, is more culturally focused. The region is home to the Batak Toba people and walks around Samosir Island may include stops at traditional Batak villages, historic stone tombs, and cultural monuments surrounded by peaceful Lake Toba waters and undulating hills. Trekking in this area offers insights into the rich cultural legacy of the Batak people while combining physical exercise with cultural immersion.

The Raw Nature of Bukit Barisan Selatan National Park

Another paradise for hikers is Bukit Barisan Selatan National Park, which stretches along Sumatra's southwest coast. The park, which is a part of the UNESCO World Heritage site, is home to some of the island's most pristine rainforests, unspoiled beaches, and endangered species including Sumatran elephants and rhinoceroses. Trekking trails here accommodate a broad variety of interests and fitness levels with a combination of animal-watching possibilities, seaside hikes, and rainforest treks.

SURFING AND WATER SPORTS

Mentawai Islands: Located off the western coast of Sumatra and reachable by ferry from Padang, the Mentawai Islands are well-known across the world among surfers. The islands are a famous surfing destination because of their excellent waves and crystal-clear seas. Waves at Lance's Right, Macaronis, and Telescopes are among the world's most reliable and demanding. When the waves are at their highest during the dry season, which runs from April to October, this is the finest time to surf this spot.

Nias Island: Known for its flawless right-hand barrel at Sorake Bay, Nias Island is another gem in Sumatra's crown. This is a strong, approachable wave that is appropriate for intermediate and experienced surfers. International surfing events are held at Nias as well, attracting surfers from all over the world. The best months to surf are May through September, which also happens to be the dry season.

South Sumatra's Krui has a range of breakers along its shoreline that are appropriate for surfers of all skill levels. Compared to the more well-known surfing spots, the region is less crowded, making it a more laid-back place to catch waves. Known for its long left-handers, Ujung Bocur, a prominent break close to Tanjung Setia Beach, is one of the most visited. April through October is when Krui has its greatest waves for surfing, with the mid-season months usually having the best action.

Sumatra's Other Water Sports

Lake Toba: This supervolcanic eruption created a caldera lake that is not only very beautiful to look at but also a

SUMATRA TRAVEL GUIDE 2024

great area to go kayaking and stand-up paddleboarding (SUP). The serene lake waters provide a serene canoeing experience, enhanced by the fascination of discovering the little islets inside the lake.

Weh Island: A diver's paradise, Weh Island is located at the northernmost point of Sumatra. The island is a great place to dive and snorkel because of its crystal-clear waters, which are home to colorful coral reefs and a wide variety of marine life. The Batee Tokong pinnacles and Rubiah Sea Garden are well-liked diving locations. Weh Island is accessible all year round, with April through November offering the finest visibility.

Alas River: The Alas River in Aceh provides thrilling white-water rafting excursions for anyone looking for heart-pounding river thrills. In addition to offering exhilarating rapids, the river passes through the Gunung Leuser National Park, offering breathtaking vistas of the rainforest. Rafting tours are available for all ability levels, from half-day outings to multi-day experiences.

DIVING AND SNORKELING SPOTS

Weh Island: A Heaven for Divers

Weh Island, off the northern point of Sumatra, is well known for its abundant marine life and crystal-clear waters, which make it a great place to dive and snorkel. The underwater geography of the island is characterized by a profusion of marine life, robust coral gardens, and volcanic rock formations. Snorkelers will love Gapang Beach and Iboih Beach, which provide easy access to spectacular coral reefs brimming with colorful fish just a short distance from the beach. At locations like Batee Tokong and the Canyon, divers may explore deeper waters. During certain seasons, encounters with bigger pelagic fish, manta rays, and even whale sharks are possible.

Pulau Banyak: An Unspoiled Beauty of an Archipelago The Banyak Islands, a collection of around 99 islands off the western coast of Sumatra, provide isolated beaches and pristine diving and snorkeling spots since they have not been overrun by tourists. A vast array of marine life, including turtles, reef sharks, and many types of tropical fish, may be found in the beautiful, turquoise seas that surround the islands. Because of the islands' isolated position, the underwater ecosystems have been conserved, offering a tranquil and personal encounter with the natural world.

Island of Nias: Beyond the Surf

Although the main attraction of Nias Island is its world-class surfing, its underwater environment is just as fascinating. The seas around Nias are home to a wide variety of marine life as well as colorful coral reefs. Snorkelers and divers may swim amid vibrant coral formations at places like Tureloto, which are home to sea turtles, schools of colorful fish, and sometimes even dolphins. Generally, there is exceptional visibility, making it possible to see the underwater extravaganza.

Mentawai Islands: A Multifaceted Marine Environment

The Mentawai Islands, which are located off the western coast of Sumatra, are a sanctuary for snorkelers and divers in addition to being a surfer's paradise. The remote location of the islands and the locals' conservation efforts have made the surrounding coral reefs among the healthiest in all of Indonesia. From small nudibranchs and vibrant reef fish to magnificent manta rays and sharks, the reefs are home to an enormous variety of marine life. Many of the island's beaches are good for snorkeling, and diving tours may take you to more isolated reefs and even some fascinating underwater rock formations.

Advice for Sumatra Snorkeling and Diving

Seasonality: From April to November, during the dry season, when sea conditions are at their calmest and visibility is at its finest, is often the optimum time to engage in underwater sports in Sumatra.

Conservation: Always engage in responsible diving and snorkeling, being sure not to disturb marine life or touch the coral. Since many ecosystems are delicate, it is important to preserve them for coming generations.

Safety: Always check your equipment before leaving the house and always dive with reliable operators. There are powerful currents in certain places, so always follow local advice and dive into your limitations.

CULTURAL FESTIVALS AND EVENTS

Danau Toba Festival

This festival is regarded by the Ministry of Tourism as the largest tourist event in the nation. The event seeks to transform North Sumatra province's Danau Toba (Lake Toba), the biggest volcanic lake in the world, into the "new" Bali. This week-long celebration, which was first conducted in the 1980s, showcases artistic performances and Batak traditional displays, including canoe races.

Festival of Krakatau

The main yearly event in the province of Lampung is the Krakatau Festival, which was first staged in 1991. It honors the memory of Mount Krakatoa's devastating eruption, which caused changes in the world's climate and filled the atmosphere with ash for days.

Every year, the event takes place between June and October.

Fashion Carnival in Jember

This event represents the apex of the modern culture of Jember, an East Javan city. The city, however modest, has captured the interest of fashion fans worldwide with its distinctive fashion carnival, whereby local designers showcase their creations on a 3.6-kilometer-long runway.

Yadnya Kasada

The Hindu Tengger people celebrate the fourteenth day of the Javanese calendar month as Sang Hyang Widhi's "offering" ritual. This ritual is held in Pura Luhur Poten, a holy site in the East Java province that is situated at the base of Mount Bromo.

Mappanretase

This celebration, which takes place in April in Pagatan, Tanah Bumbu Regency, South Kalimantan province, is a way for the Bugis Pagatan people to express their gratitude to God for all of their benefits. The Bugis term "mappanretasi" means "feeding the sea." Fishing boats with gifts, including bananas, sticky rice, or chickens, sail to the beach's center before the procession resumes.

Tomohon Flower Festival

This flower festival was first hosted in the lovely hill town of Tomohon in the province of North Sulawesi in 2006. The government decided to make it an annual event starting in 2014. Usually, it attracts tourists from abroad.

Four main activities comprise the festival: displays of floriculture, art and culture performances, the Queen of Flowers, and the Tournament of Flowers. The Tournament of Flowers is a grand flower procession that travels through Tomohon's principal streets in fragrant and beautiful cars.

Festival of Baliem Valley

This event takes place in August in the province of Papua's Baliem Valley. For a joyous mock battle, it gathers all the various tribes from the Baliem Valley and the highlands of Wamena, including the Dani, Lani, and Yali tribes. The tribes saw battle as a sign of fertility and wealth in addition to legitimate combat. Professional photographers have been drawn to this event in particular because they produce some amazing tribal shots.

CULTURAL AND HISTORICAL SITES

TRADITIONAL VILLAGES AND AND CULTURAL TOURS

North Sumatra's Mysterious Batak Kingdoms

The ancient Batak kingdoms have left behind a rich heritage of architectural and cultural gems in the highlands of North Sumatra. The distinctive boat-shaped roofs and intricate carvings of the traditional "Toba Batak houses" and stone graves serve as a tribute to the Batak people's distinct cultural identity. Situated in the center of the world's biggest volcanic lake, Lake Toba, the town of Ambarita on Samosir Island is especially famous for its collection of antique stone seats and tables, which were previously used by the community elders for council and justice-giving.

The Banda Aceh Grand Mosque

The Baiturrahman Grand Mosque, located in Banda Aceh, Sumatra's northernmost point, is a representation of tenacity and religious devotion. The mosque was originally erected in the twelfth century, but following a disastrous fire in the late nineteenth century, the Dutch rebuilt it in a palatial manner. With its two towering minarets and seven black domes, this spectacular white monument is a tribute to Aceh's rich Islamic tradition and how it survived the 2004 tsunami that destroyed most of the surrounding region.

Heritage of Dutch Colonialism in Medan

The biggest city in Sumatra, Medan, is known for its remarkable collection of Dutch colonial buildings, which are a holdover from its days as a major tobacco trading hub. Constructed in 1888 by the Sultan of Deli, the Maimoon Palace is a unique and sumptuous monument that combines Moorish, Indian, and Spanish architectural styles with Malay cultural features. Another noteworthy location is the Tjong A Fie Mansion, a sumptuous home with a Victorian and Chinese style that was constructed in the late 19th century by a Chinese businessman and philanthropist.

The Padang Old Town

West Sumatra's capital, Padang, is widely known for its remarkably intact colonial old town, where one can see clear traces of Dutch architectural influence in the houses lining the streets. The historic harbor district still echoes the busy bustle of spice dealers, indicative of the city's status as a major trading port. The Adityawarman Museum, based in a Dutch colonial structure, gives insights into the region's Minangkabau culture and history.

Bengkulu Fort Marlborough

One of the most important British colonial fortifications in Indonesia, Fort Marlborough is located in the city of Bengkulu on the western coast of Sumatra. The fort, which was constructed in the early 1700s to protect against Dutch and French armies, stands as a powerful reminder of the European power struggles in the area thanks to its high walls and advantageous position overlooking the sea. It is now a historical monument where tourists may explore its tunnels, bastions, and traces of its colonial history.

HISTORICAL SITES AND COLONIAL HERITAGE

The West Sumatra Minangkabau Villages

Native to the lush highlands of West Sumatra, the Minangkabau are distinguished by their matrilineal culture in which family names and property are handed down via female lineage. Pariangan, a village tucked away at the base of Mount Marapi, provides an insight into traditional Minangkabau life. The unique Minangkabau architecture, with its arching, buffalo-horn-shaped roofs signifying wealth and societal peace, is marveled at by tourists here. Cultural excursions might include tastings of the rich, fiery Minangkabau cuisine that is well-known across Indonesia, as well as visits to local houses and performances of traditional music and dance.

The Communities of Batak in North Sumatra

Not only is Lake Toba the biggest volcanic lake in the world, but it is also the home of the Batak Toba people. Traditional settlements like Ambarita and Simanindo on Samosir Island, within the lake, provide intriguing insights into Batak culture. The intricately carved wooden homes, referred to as "Rumah Bolon," and the old stone graves depict a very religious society. Concerts of Toba Batak music, which combines the rhythmic beat of the gondang drums with the lyrical sounds of the hasapi (a traditional lute), are often included in cultural tours. Additionally, visitors may discover the significance of ulos fabric in Batak culture as well as the traditional weaving methods used by the people.

Bengkulu Rejang Lebong

The less well-known traditional villages of the Rejang people may be explored by tourists in the Rejang Lebong Regency of Bengkulu. This region is renowned for its colorful events and celebrations, many of which include elaborate costumes, folk music, and group dances. Particularly the Serawai ethnic group is renowned for its exquisite weaving and exquisite traditional homes. Cultural trips to these communities provide a chance to see customary Rejang rites and learn about their intricate belief systems and social structures.

The Villages of Kerinci Seblat National Park

Many villages encircle the enormous Kerinci Seblat National Park, which is home to the critically endangered Sumatran tiger. Here, tourists may see the healthy coexistence of Sumatra's inhabitants with their natural surroundings. Living adjacent to the park, ethnic groups like the Kerinci provide guided tours that teach guests about the traditional agricultural, honey-gathering, and conservation methods used by the community in addition to seeing the area's abundant biodiversity. These excursions provide a unique viewpoint on the difficulties and benefits of being close to one of the most biodiverse areas on Earth.

FOOD AND CULINARY EXPERIENCES

SUMATRAN CUISINE

Pempek

Pempek, an inexpensive and tasty snack prepared from a surimi (fish paste) of mackerel flesh mixed with tapioca flour and spices, is highly recommended by the natives of Palembang. After pempek is boiled or fried, it's served with cake, a dark, spicy-sweet sauce, and either noodles, rice, or sliced cucumber on the side.

Pempek kapal selam, which is essentially a boiled egg fashioned like an Indonesian scotch egg, pempek bulat, which is formed like little balls, and pempek lenjer, which is a long, sausage-shaped pempek that is often sliced into morsels before serving, are just a few of the unexpectedly many ways that this simple street meal may be prepared.

Pempek Lince (Jl. Tugumulyo No.2398, Kota Palembang) or Pempek are the places to sample it.

Vico (D. I, Palembang, Jalan Veteran No. 8B)

Medan's Lontong Sayur

Lontong are very symbolic rice cakes. Every significant city in Java and Sumatra has a lontong-based meal, and because of its cultural ties to Lebaran, Indonesia's Eid'l Fitr season, Medan residents love eating it as a way to break their fast or celebrate Eid Ul Fitri.

After Lebaran, when you dine with the locals, you should try Medan's take on lontong sayur, which is a soup prepared with coconut milk, fermented bean paste, and shrimp, along with pieces of rice cake and veggies. Additional toppings include chayote, long beans, jackfruit, carrots, hard boiled eggs, and keropok, which are crispy fritters.

Lontong Warintek (Jalan Dr Mansur, Medan) or Lontong are the places to sample it.

Kak Lin is located in front of SMA 1 Medan on Jalan Teuku Cik di Tiro No. 76.

Padang Soto

Despite the absence of coconut milk in Javanese or Madurese soto, the Minang people of Padang maintain that their version of beef soup is better. Traditional spices, which give the soup a punch you can taste before you bring the spoon to your lips, are how Minang chefs enhance their soto.

Rice noodles, potato fritters, and meat are the fundamental ingredients of Soto Padang. The meat may be served as dendeng balado, the regional version of beef jerky; some diners pair soto padang with ketupat, or rice cakes, or with hard boiled eggs.

Where to try it: Soto Minang Roda Jaya (Jl. Tepi Pasang No. 67, Padang) or Soto Garuda (Parman Kelurahan No. 110, Padang).

Tangkap Ayam

Ayam tangkap, a highly regionalized fried chicken dish from Aceh, uses pandanus, curry leaves, and lemongrass in addition to a marinade made with spices found in the area. The recipe asks for marinated free-range chicken, which is then diced into morsels and deep-fried to produce a crunchy, savory meal that goes well with soy sauce and white rice. Typically, ayam tangkap is served in big portions suitable for gatherings of three to five people.

The rather dark sense of humor of the Acehnese has been amused by the "messy" appearance of the fried chicken.

The term "ayam tsunami" (tsunami chicken) is popular among the locals, evoking memories of the catastrophic devastation caused by the 2004 Indian Ocean tsunami.

Try it at Ayam Pramugari (Jl. Blang Bintang Lama, Banda Aceh) or Warung Makan Hasan 3 (Cabang Kreung Cut, Banda Aceh).

Sate Padang

Padang chose to introduce two of its versions of traditional Indonesian BBQ into the food industry as if one interpretation wasn't enough. You may choose between Padang Panjang and Padang Pariaman while eating in Padang. In the former, a medium amount of spices and a brownish-yellow sauce with hints of turmeric are used. The latter has a sauce that is more intense and reddish-brown.

As opposed to the chicken or beef satay more in keeping with the rest of Indonesia, both varieties of satay employ buffalo meat. Along with spices like cumin, turmeric, galangal, and coriander, beef, cow tongue, and offal are first boiled before being skewered and cooked to perfection. The dish is then served with rice or ketupat rice cake with spicy cassava chips on the side.

TOP RESTAURANTS

Marriott Café

The Marriott Cafe in Medan serves a variety of Asian, Indian, and Western meals all day long. The waitstaff is kind and helpful, and the buffet is an excellent place for people to experience a wide range of diverse dishes. The restaurant offers alcohol and has wheelchair access.

Jl. North Sumatra 20111, North Sumatra Putri Hijau No. 10, Kesawan, Medan Barat, Medan City, Indonesia

Jade Dining Establishment

Lokasari Baru is a straightforward, spotless restaurant with affordable rates and welcoming, cozy service for all patrons. Lokasari Baru serves a wide range of specialties, including cha kangkung, cap chai, soybean sauce, fried chicken with fried onions, and many more mouthwatering seafood meals and cool beverages. The room is open, and it's a tad loud and packed. Don't hesitate to go there and experience the tastiest cuisine Padang has to offer while dining with loved ones.

Address of the place: Jl. Warung Lokasari Baru. Berok Nipah, Kec., Nipah No. 34 C. Padang Bar., Kota Padang, Indonesia's Sumatera Barat

The Thirty-Six Cafe

The Thirty-Six Café - This lovely café has plant-decorated interior and outdoor sitting sections as well as a stunning décor. Its menu features a variety of delectable Asian and foreign foods, such as grilled beef sandwiches and curd pancakes. It serves a wide variety of delectable beverages and pastries.

Location address: Jl. No. 36 Multatuli, Hamdan, Kec. Sumatera Utara 20151, Medan Maimun, Kota Medan, Indonesia

Restaurant Garuda

Garuda Restaurant: This restaurant is well-known for its Padang rice, which is served with roughly 20 little dishes loaded with different kinds of curries, fish, veggies, and sauces. If you want to experience some of the most delectable local foods in Medan, don't hesitate to come.

Location: Silalas, Kec., Jalan Haji Adam Malik D/H Glugur Bypass No. 14. Indonesia; Medan Bar., Kota Medan, Sumatera Utara 20114.

Tabona Dining Establishment

Tabona Restaurant: Since 1983, Tabuna Restaurant has focused on providing a wide variety of classic curry meals. You may have a curry meal with rice or noodles, for instance, or chicken or beef. Along with a large selection of hot and cold beverages, it is well-known for its welcoming personnel and excellent service.

Location address: Jl. No. 17 Mangkubumi, A U R, Kec. Sumatera Utara 20151, Medan Maimun, Kota Medan, Indonesia

The Vegetarian Restaurant in Medan

Medan Vegetarian Restaurant: If you like vegetarian cuisine, you should check out the Meydan Vegetarian Restaurant, which offers a variety of mouthwatering regional vegetarian delicacies. Along with its lovely contemporary design and cozy ambiance, this restaurant is known for its excellent service.

Location address: JL. No. 23A-25, Airlangga, Madras Hulu, Kec. Indonesia, Medan Polonia, Kota Medan, Sumatera Utara 20151,

ACCOMMODATION

TOP HOTELS

1. EcoTrip Cabins in Bukit Lawang

Location: In Bukit Lawang, North Sumatra, close to the Gunung Leuser National Park entrance.

Price: From around $40 per night forward.

Overview: For those who like the outdoors and an exciting trip, EcoTravel Cottages Bukit Lawang offers eco-friendly lodging. Located next to the verdant Gunung Leuser National Park and on the banks of the Bohorok River, visitors may experience the peace and beauty of the rainforest. To reduce their negative environmental effects, the cottages are constructed using traditional materials and methods. The helpful and courteous staff arranges river tubing, cultural excursions, and guided forest hikes for guests to see orangutans. With an emphasis on using foods that are organic and sustainably produced, the on-site restaurant serves a range of regional and international cuisines.

2. Tabo Cottages

Location: Samosir Island in North Sumatra near Lake Toba.

Cost: About $50 per night to start.

Overview: Nestled in the heart of Lake Toba, the biggest volcanic lake in the world, Tabo Cottages is situated on the charming island of Samosir. This family-run resort offers a tranquil haven with breathtaking views of Lake Toba by combining traditional Batak architecture with contemporary amenities. There are many different types of lodging available to guests, ranging from basic rooms to roomy villas with their balconies. The resort has a restaurant providing delectable regional and international cuisine, a private beach area, and a swimming pool. To make your stay at this picturesque lakeside retreat even more memorable, cultural tours, traditional Batak dance performances, and trips to neighboring destinations may be planned.

3. Paradiso Village in Cubadak

Location: In West Sumatra, close to Padang, is Cubadak Island.

Cost: Nightly rates, which include meals and activities, begin at around $150.

Overview: Cubadak Paradiso Village is a boutique resort that provides a luxurious getaway in a tropical paradise. It is tucked away on the quiet island of Cubadak. With only 12 bungalows and 1 family villa, the resort makes sure that every visitor has a quiet and personal stay. The bungalows have contemporary conveniences mixed with a classic decor.

4. Bukit Lawang Jungle Inn

Location: North Sumatra's Bukit Lawang, near the Gunung Leuser National Park.

Cost: Nightly rates begin at around $30.

Overview: Offering a true rainforest experience, rainforest Inn Bukit Lawang is located on the border of Gunung Leuser National Park. This little lodge is well known for its distinctive construction, which combines natural elements into the design of the rooms and communal spaces. Certain rooms are equipped with naturally occurring rock formations and waterfalls, resulting in a very captivating jungle ambiance. From their balconies, guests can take in the sounds of the river and surrounding animals. The hotel provides a variety of environmentally friendly activities, such as river tubing, cultural visits to nearby communities, and guided hikes into the national park to see orangutans in their native habitat. Fresh, regional ingredients are used to make a range of regional and international cuisines served at the on-site restaurant.

5. Iboih Hotel

Location: Pulau Weh, Aceh, Iboih Beach.

Price: Roughly $25 per night to start.

Overview: Located on the picturesque coastline of Pulau Weh, a tiny volcanic island renowned for its immaculate beaches and great diving locations, Iboih Inn provides a tranquil beachside retreat. The inn offers straightforward yet cozy lodging options, from standard rooms to seaside cottages. The luxury and seclusion that each room offers enable visitors to decompress and wind down to the sound of the waves. With its dive center, the inn provides PADI-certified diving instruction along with expeditions to some of the greatest underwater locations in the area, where guests may discover a wide variety of marine life and vivid coral reefs. There are additional options for island hopping cruises, fishing, and snorkeling. Delicious local seafood and a variety of Indonesian and Western meals are served at the restaurant at Iboih Inn, making it the ideal place to eat while taking in breathtaking views of the sea.

PRACTICAL INFORMATION

HEALTH AND SAFETY TIPS

Sumatra's tropical environment makes it prone to dehydration, so be sure to drink plenty of bottled water. When purchasing street food, use caution and choose vendors that prepare the dish right in front of you. Use authorized taxis or reliable transportation services at all times for your protection, particularly while visiting far-flung locations. Keep a watch on your surroundings, especially in busy areas, to prevent small-time theft.

Keep a safe distance and show respect for wildlife while in natural regions. Beautiful but possibly hazardous creatures may be found in Sumatra's jungles. Hiring a local guide may enhance your outdoor experience and ensure your safety while exploring new areas whether hiking or participating in other outdoor sports.

Overcoming Communication Gaps in Sumatra

Even though Bahasa Indonesia is the official language, the many ethnic groups that make up Sumatra speak a wide range of regional tongues. Limited English competence may exist, especially outside of large towns and popular tourist destinations. Gaining proficiency in a few fundamental Bahasa Indonesia phrases will greatly improve your communication with locals. Starters like "Selamat pagi" (good morning), "Terima kasih" (thank you), and "Berapa harganya?" (how much is this?) are helpful.

Language barriers may also be overcome via technology. Apps for translation may make talks more complicated and aid in reading menus and signage. Having an app handy or carrying a compact phrasebook may improve your trip by facilitating communication with locals and facilitating day-to-day activities.

CURRENCY, PAYMENTS AND TIPPING

In Sumatra, the official currency is the Indonesian Rupiah (IDR). Carrying enough cash is advisable since it's the preferred form of payment in many regions of the island, particularly in rural areas and small towns. While they may be hard to find in rural places, ATMs are common in metropolitan areas. Most upscale hotels, restaurants, and retail establishments take credit cards, but it's important to check in advance.

Although it is not customarily anticipated, tips are given for excellent service in Indonesia. If there is no service fee, it is considerate to round up the total or leave a little tip (5–10%). You may choose to leave a tip for drivers and tour guides that expresses your gratitude for their assistance.

Customs and Manners of the People of Sumatra

It's important to respect the traditions and customs of the people you visit in Sumatra. When attending places of worship, wear modest clothing; covering one's knees and shoulders is advised. When entering a person's house or other inside area, always take off your shoes.

A little bow or a nod is customary while greeting, and handshakes are often saved for initial introductions. Since the left hand is seen as unclean, use the right hand for eating and passing objects. Recognize that showing love in public is not appropriate in more conservative settings.

Since peace and civility are highly valued by Sumatrans, they always greet problems with a smile and tolerance.

Gaining an appreciation for these subtle cultural differences may greatly enhance your trip to Sumatra by fostering stronger ties with the locals and enhancing your understanding of their distinctive way of life.

ITINERARIES AND DAY TRIPS

SAMPLE ITINERARIES FOR SHORT AND LONG VISITS

Day 1: Bukit Lawang - Medan

- Morning: Get to North Sumatra's capital, Medan. Investigate the Grand Mosque and Maimoon Palace.

- Afternoon: Drive for about three to four hours to Bukit Lawang.

- Evening: Check into your lodging. A splendid evening was spent by the Bohorok River.

Day 2: Jungle Trekking in Bukit Lawang

- Early in the morning: Set off on a full-day guided forest walk in Gunung Leuser National Park to see wildlife, including orangutans.

- Afternoon: Continue your jungle exploration as your guide prepares lunch for you to eat in the wild.

In the evening, go back to Bukit Lawang. Free night to unwind or go around the village.

Day 3: Lake Toba to Bukit Lawang

- Morning: Make the 6- to 7-hour trip to Lake Toba, the biggest volcanic lake in the world.

- Arrive at Parapat in the afternoon and board the boat to Samosir Island.

- Evening: Arrive at your Samosir Island lodging. Take in the views of Lake Toba while dining.

Day 4: Samosir Island Exploration

- Morning: See historic stone tombs and traditional homes by visiting traditional Batak villages including Tomok and Ambarita.

- Afternoon: Take a stroll around Samosir on your bike, kayak, or beside the lake.

- In the evening, take in a cultural show or sample some of the island's cuisine.

Day 5: Medan to Lake Toba

- In the morning, travel to Medan and return via ferry to Parapat.

- Afternoon: Visit the Rahmat International Wildlife Museum & Gallery or do some last-minute shopping in Medan's local marketplaces.

- Evening: We leave Medan.

An Example Schedule for a Prolonged Trip to Sumatra (10–14 Days)

Day 1–2: Bukit Lawang - Medan

- Adhere to the brief visit itinerary for Days 1 and 2, which includes seeing Medan and going on a forest excursion to Bukit Lawang.

Day 3–4: Berastagi to Bukit Lawang

- In the morning, go to Berastagi, a town in the highlands renowned for its fruit markets and chilly weather.

- Day 4: Take a morning hike up the Sibayak Volcano and spend the day at the nearby hot springs.

Days 5-7: Samosir Island and Lake Toba

- Add the excursion to Lake Toba from the condensed schedule to days five and six.

- Day 7: See more of the island; you would like to hire a motorcycle to see more remote waterfalls and traditional communities.

Day 8–9: Bukittinggi and Padang

- In the morning: Take a plane or car to Padang, and from there go to the Minangkabau highlands village of Bukittinggi.

- Visit the Pagaruyung Palace, the Japanese Tunnels, and the Sianok Canyon. Savor some Minangkabau food.

Day 10: The Harau Valley

- A day's journey to the rice fields and cliffs of Harau Valley. Appreciate hiking and exploring the nearby communities.

Day 11–12: Islands of Mentawai

Morning: Return to Padang, where you'll board a ferry to the Mentawai Islands.

- Take in the beaches, surf, and native Mentawai culture for two days.

Day 13: Go back to the Padang

- AM: Head back to Padang. Discover the city by going to places like Padang Beach and the Adityawarman Museum.

- Evening: Savor a goodbye meal that highlights Padang cuisine, which is renowned for its diverse and flavorful dishes.

Day 14: Padang departure

- Leave Padang, or stay longer to see more of the undiscovered beauties of Sumatra.

DAY TRIPS AND EXCURSIONS

Samosir Island and Lake Toba from Medan

The biggest volcanic lake in the world, Lake Toba, is accessible from Medan and provides a glimpse into the rich Batak culture. The journey takes about a day. The trip itself is a sight to see, going through the Sumatran highlands. After arriving in Parapat, you may go by ferry to Samosir Island, which is situated in the center of Lake Toba. Discover the quaint Batak settlements of Tomok and Tuktuk, marvel at historic stone tombs, and take in traditional Batak dance performances all around you. The calm ambience of the lake offers an ideal setting for unwinding and introspection.

Batu Katak and the Landak River from Bukit Lawang

Batu Katak, a lesser-known region that's just a short drive from Bukit Lawang, provides a true rainforest experience away from the people. Trekking through the jungle and seeing animals like orangutans, Thomas leaf monkeys, and other bird species are all possible activities for a day excursion to this location. The trip might continue to the Landak River, where guests can bathe in the refreshing water or enjoy tubing through the serene scenery. For those who want to get in touch with nature and discover Sumatra's amazing biodiversity, this trip is perfect.

Harau Valley and Minangkabau Villages are reached from Padang.

Journeying to the Harau Valley from Padang exposes visitors to the breathtaking inner vistas of Sumatra. The valley is well-known for its serene waterfalls, verdant rice fields, and majestic granite cliffs. In this charming environment, guests may go trekking, rock climbing, or just have picnics. Visits to neighboring Minangkabau communities, including Pagaruyung, where the traditional dwellings have distinctive roofs fashioned like buffalo horns, are another option for the trip. Here, visitors may experience some of the well-known regional food while also learning about the Minangkabau people's matrilineal lifestyle and rich cultural traditions.

Pulau Weh, from Banda Aceh

Pulau Weh, with its lovely beaches, crystal-clear seas, and colorful coral reefs, is a tranquil getaway only a short boat trip from Banda Aceh. This trip is ideal for diving, snorkeling, or just taking in the laid-back vibe of the island. Underwater fans will find the island's varied marine life to be a delight, and breathtaking panoramic views may be had from its picturesque locations, such as the Kilometer Nol, which is Indonesia's westernmost point. Pulau Weh is a great day trip destination for those who want to relax by the sea because of its natural beauty and laid-back vibe.

Investigating Beyond: National Park of Kerinci Seblat

A day excursion into the center of Kerinci Seblat National Park provides an unmatched chance for those with more adventure to see Sumatra's immense wildness. It is the island's biggest national park and is home to elephants, rhinos, and the rare Sumatran tiger. Hiking routes lead to high-altitude Lake Gunung Tujuh, surrounded by deep rainforest, as well as hidden waterfalls and hot springs. A day's journey offers an exciting introduction to Sumatra's untamed heart, even if it just scrapes the surface of what the park has to offer.

CONCLUSION

As our fascinating voyage throughout Sumatra comes to an end, we consider how far it has brought us from the busy streets of Medan to the tranquil waters of Lake Toba and the heart of the verdant Gunung Leuser National Park. This book has tried to be your travel companion, bringing to light moments that encapsulate the spirit of this amazing island as you explore Sumatra's varied landscapes and rich cultures.

Emotions in Sumatra are as vibrant as the sunsets over its beaches. It's where the most ordinary encounters become life-changing ones, whether it's the excitement of seeing an orangutan in the wild, the warmth of a Minangkabau grin, or the peace of a Batak hamlet near Lake Toba. These recollections serve as a constant reminder of the deep bonds we develop with the places and people we encounter on our travels.

We've embraced pragmatism to explore Sumatra's delights, from taking health precautions in the tropics to respectfully navigating local traditions. But what unlocks Sumatra's riches are an open mind, a willingness to deviate from the usual route, and a readiness to immerse oneself in the experience.

I appreciate you letting this book serve as your entryway to Sumatra. This area of undiscovered treasures and unwritten tales has a wealth of marvels waiting to be discovered; the stories recounted and the landscapes explored are simply a taste of what is ahead. Sumatra invites you to keep traveling, to come back, and to explore even more of its varied cultures and secret nooks because of its inexhaustible mysteries and charms.

Allow Sumatra's attitude to motivate you to welcome adventure, explore the uncharted, and value the world's natural splendor and cultural diversity. May Sumatra's memories cling to you in your heart like the call of a forest, beckoning you back into its spellbinding embrace. So let us separate with a vow, not of farewell but of fresh adventure, our hearts full of memories and our eyes fixed on the horizon. May your travels be safe, your experiences great, and your soul unafraid of the breadth of the globe to explore till we meet again.

With fondness and good vibes.

Printed in Great Britain
by Amazon

42371453R00056